Fairy Dreams

Coloring Book

by Molly Harrison

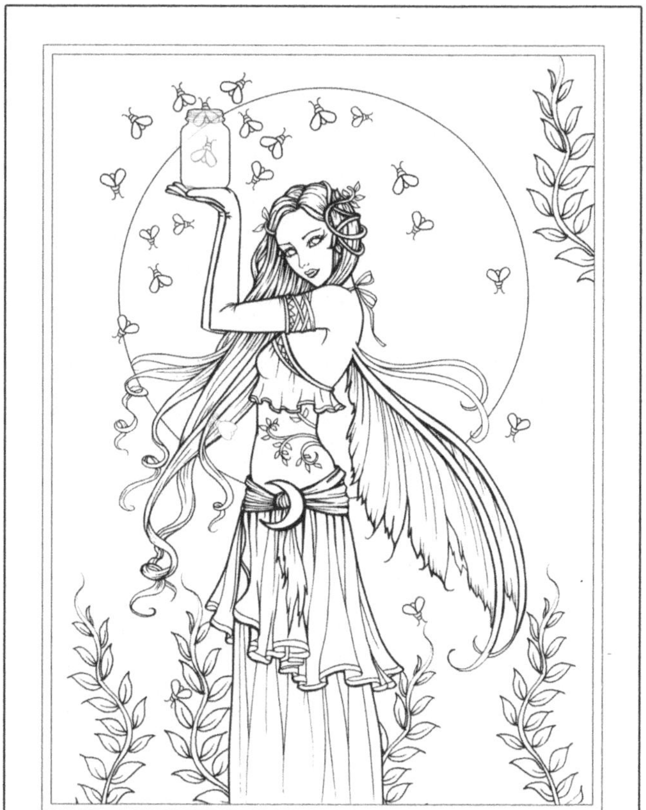

www.mollyharrisonart.com

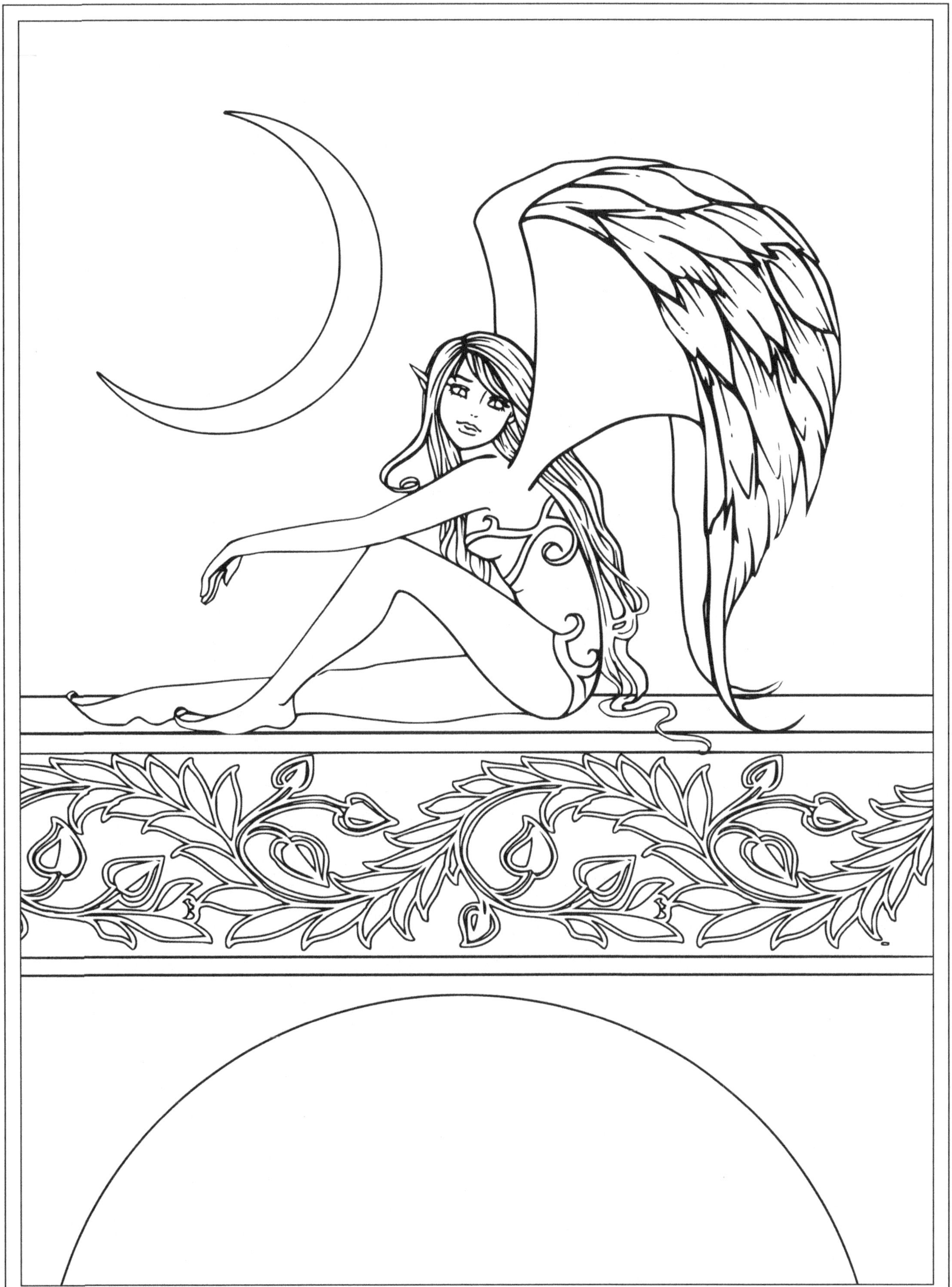

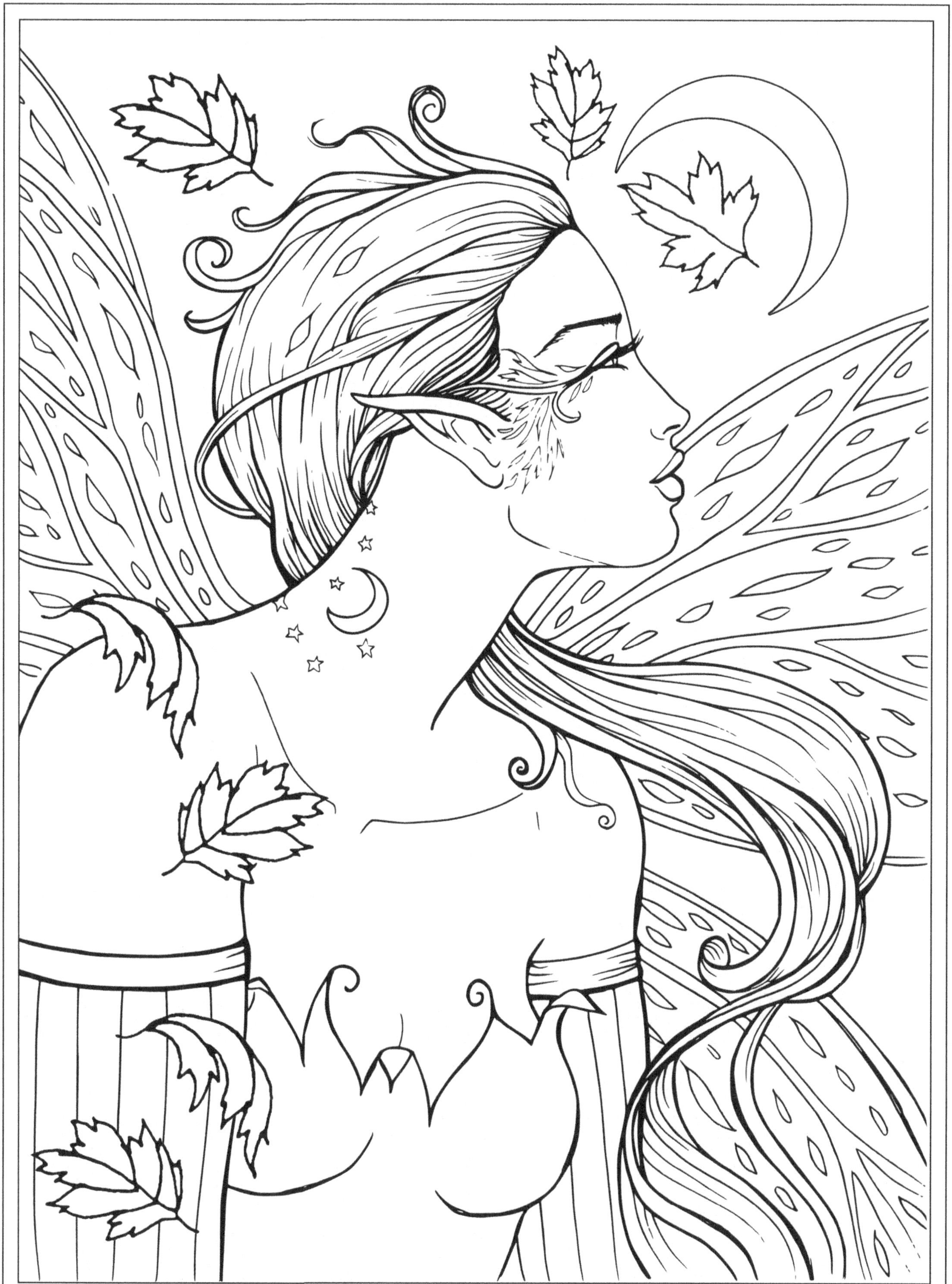

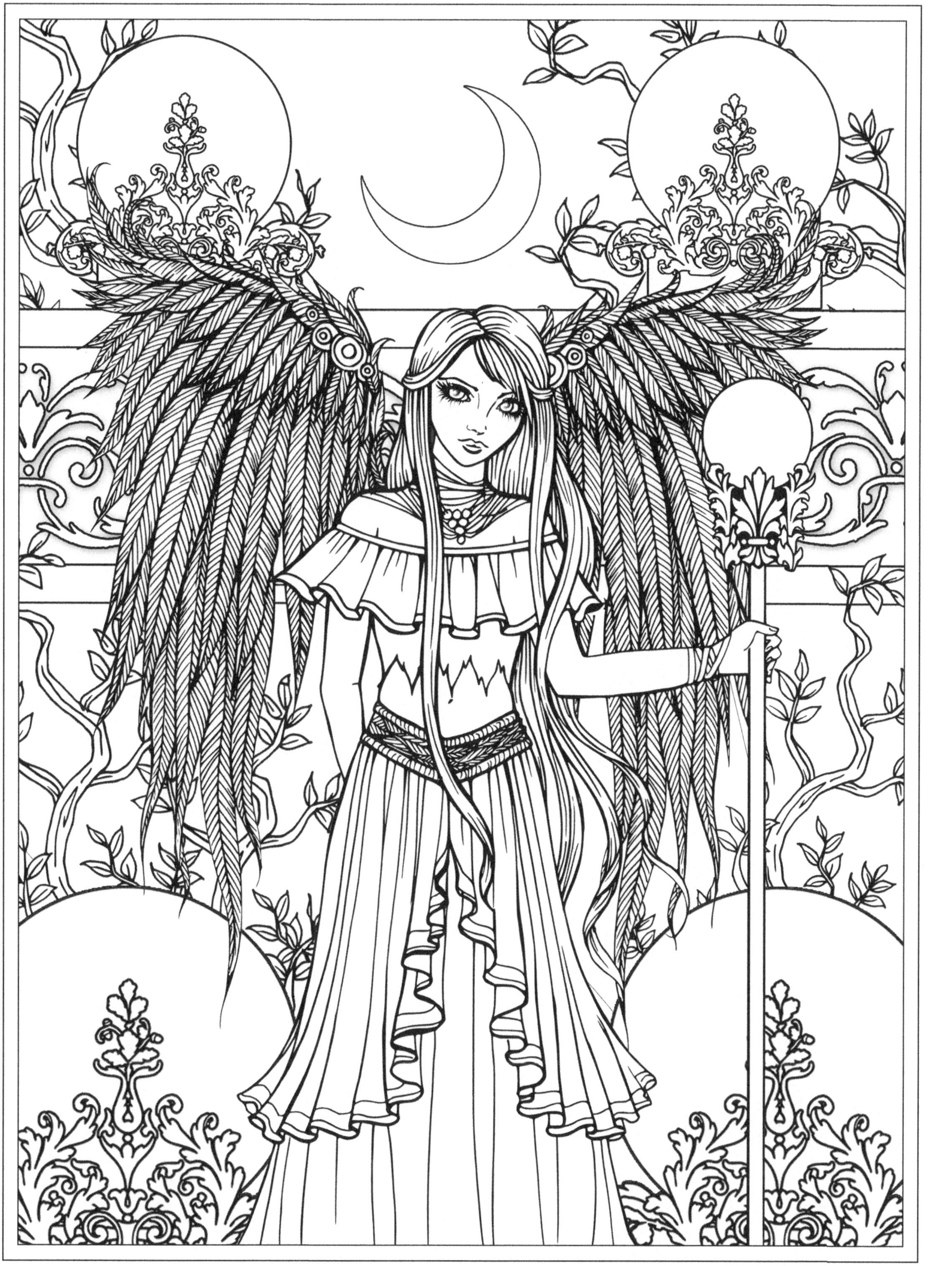

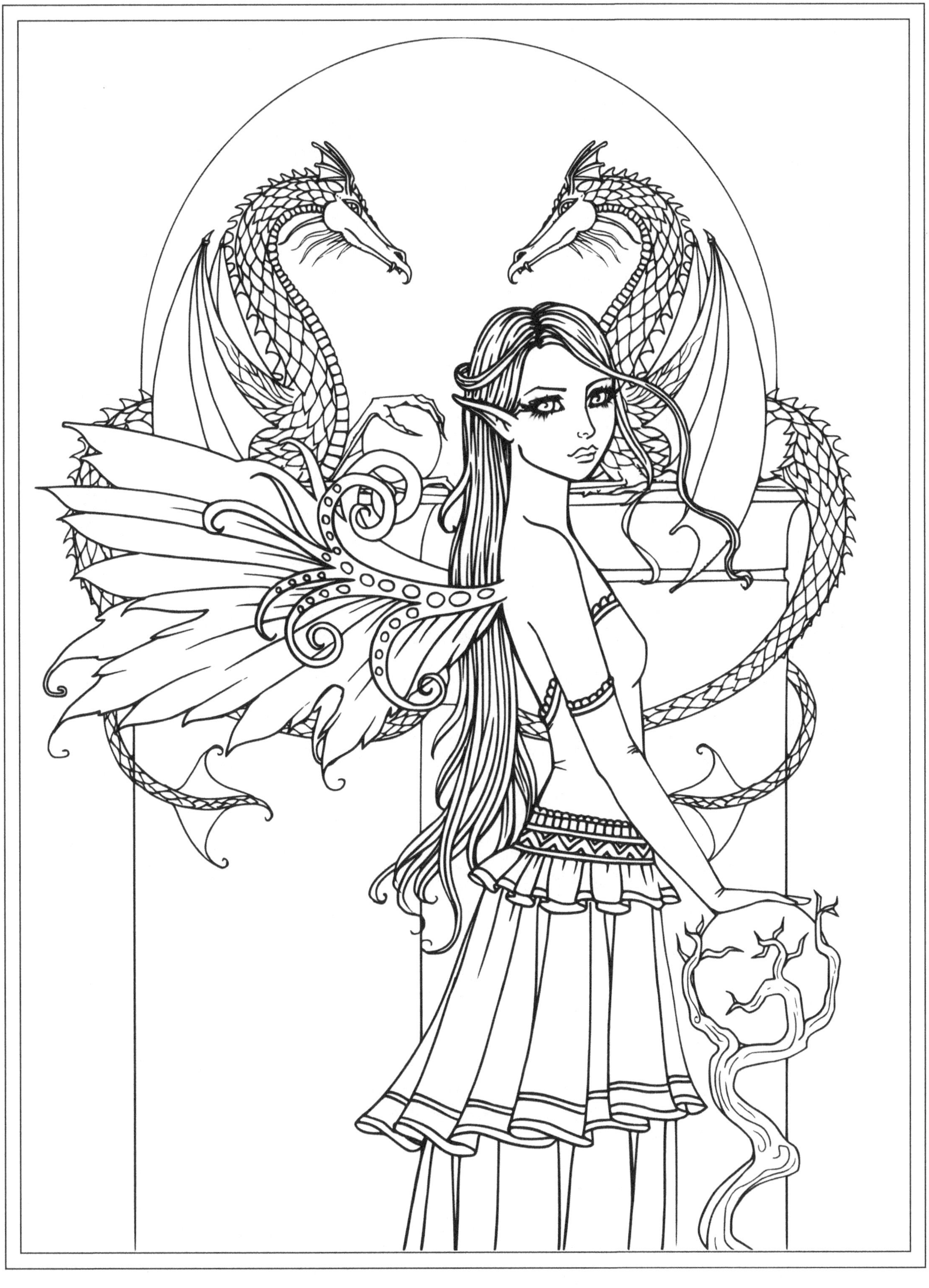

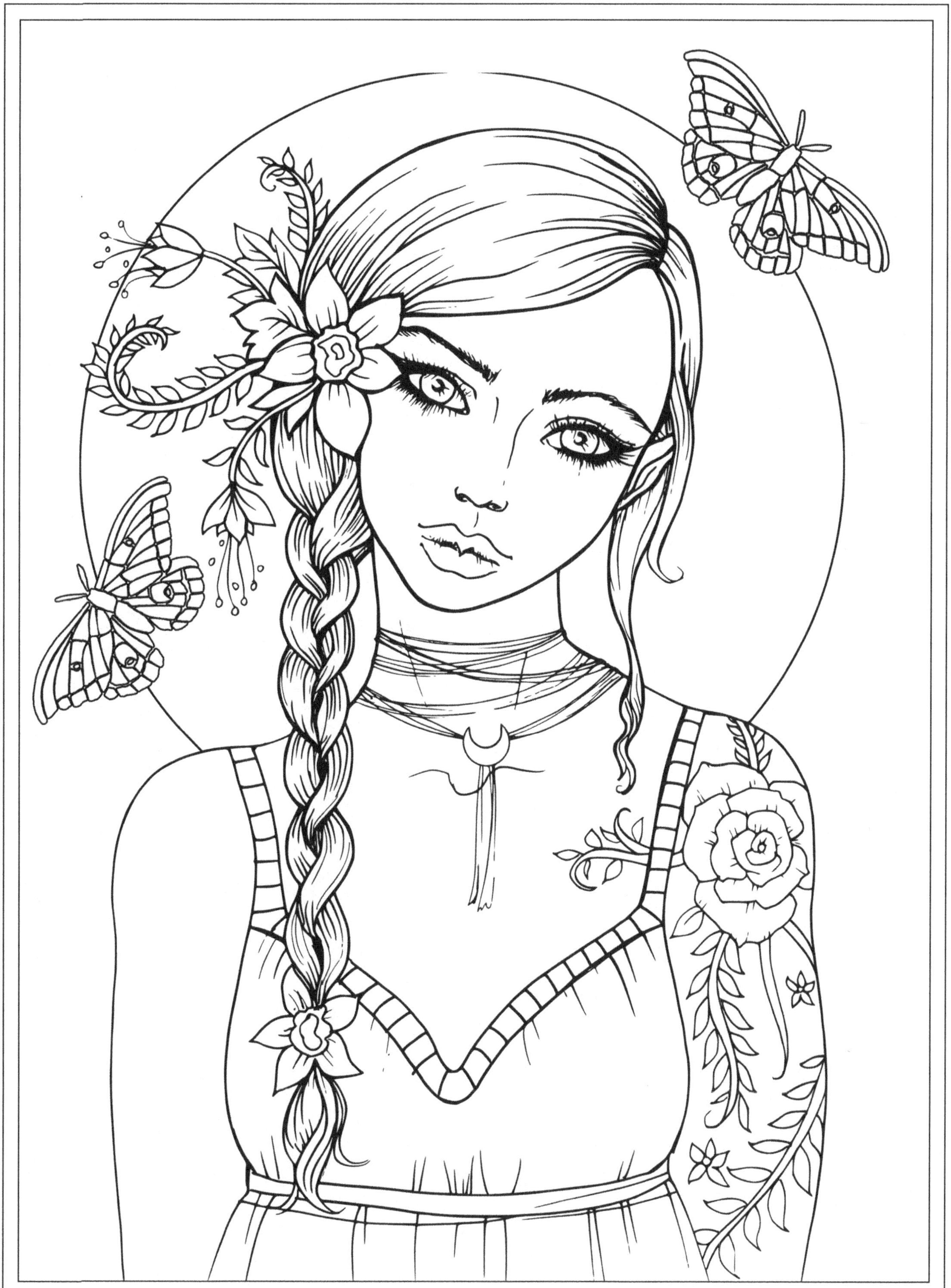

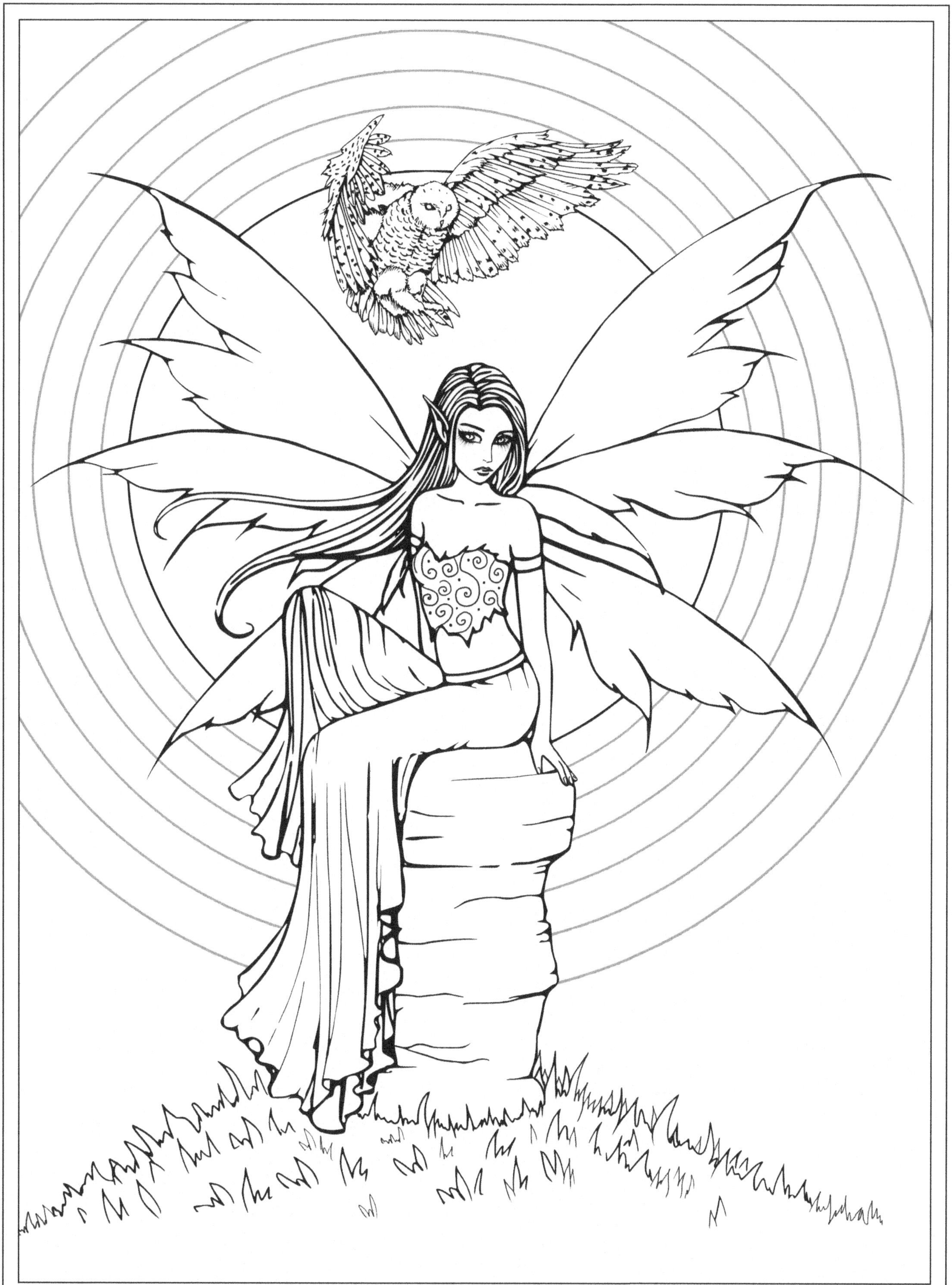

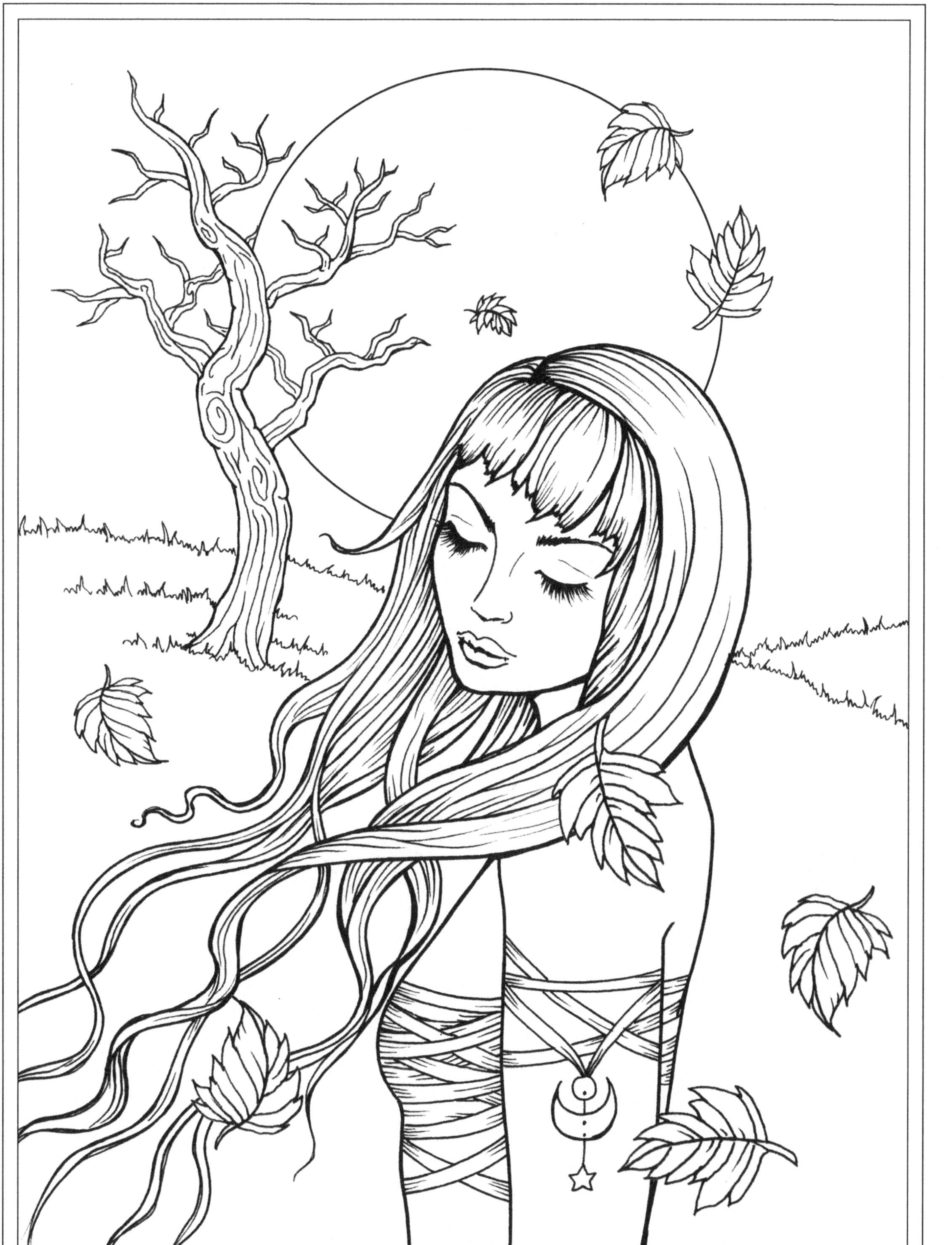

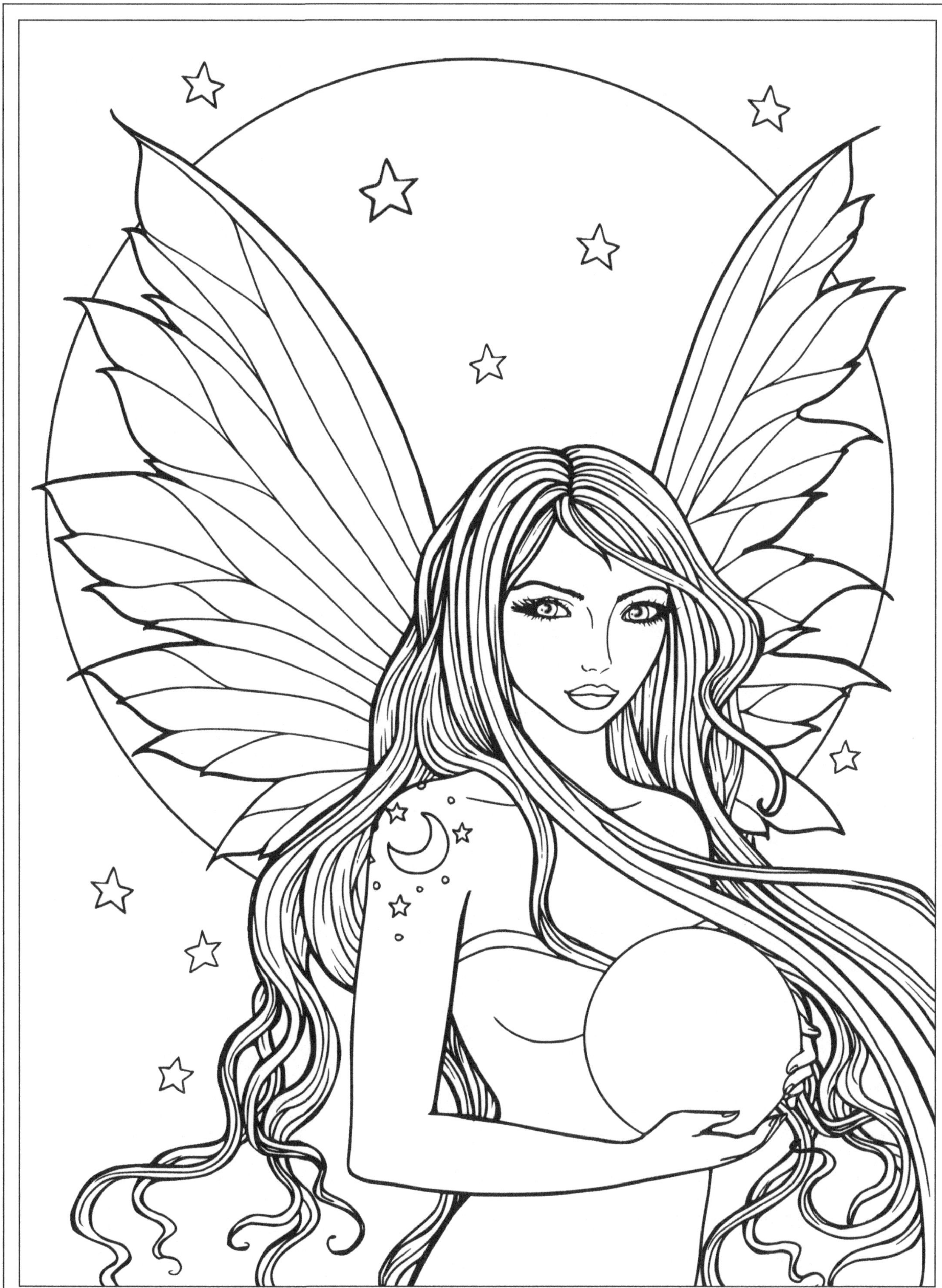

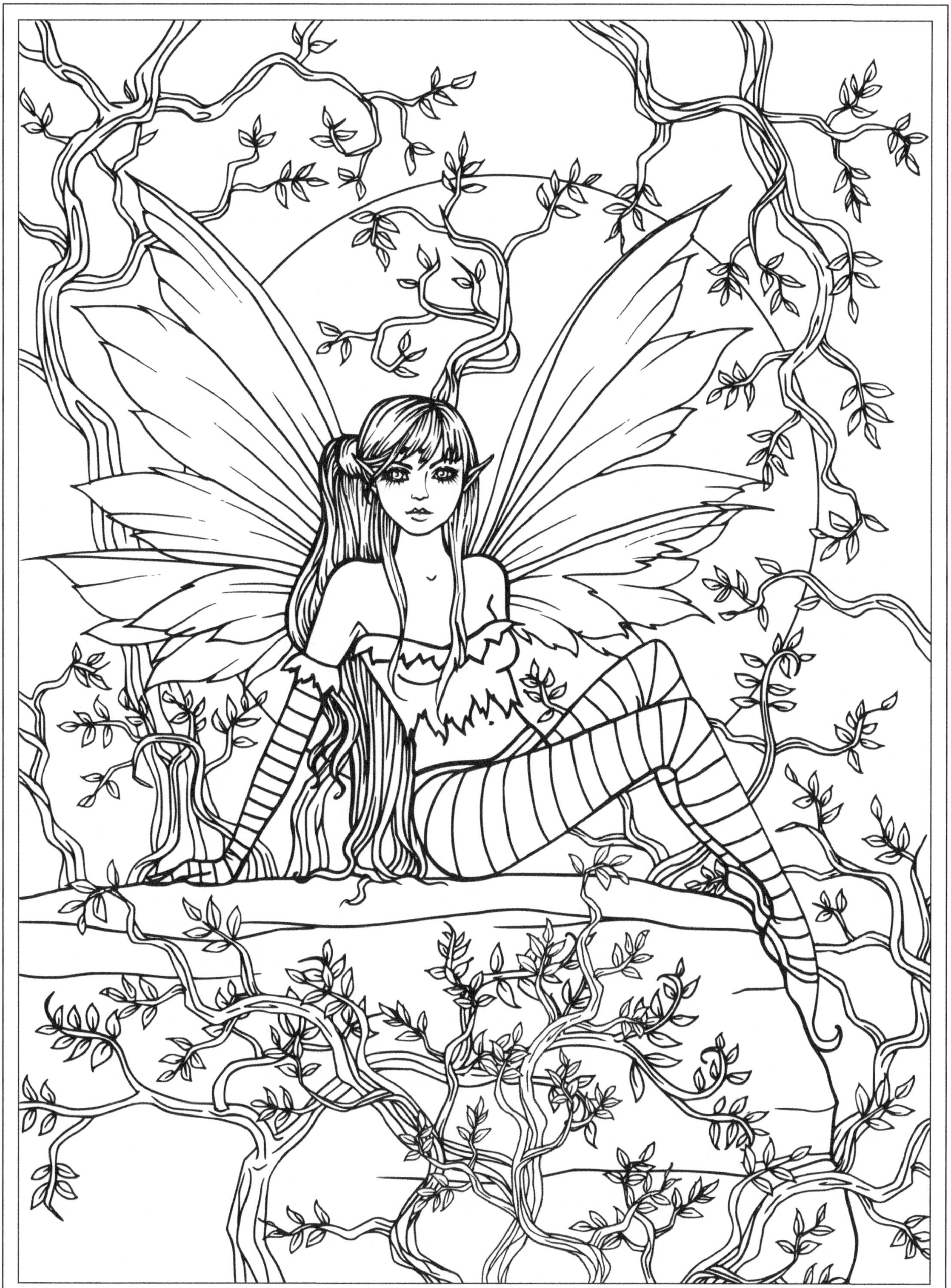

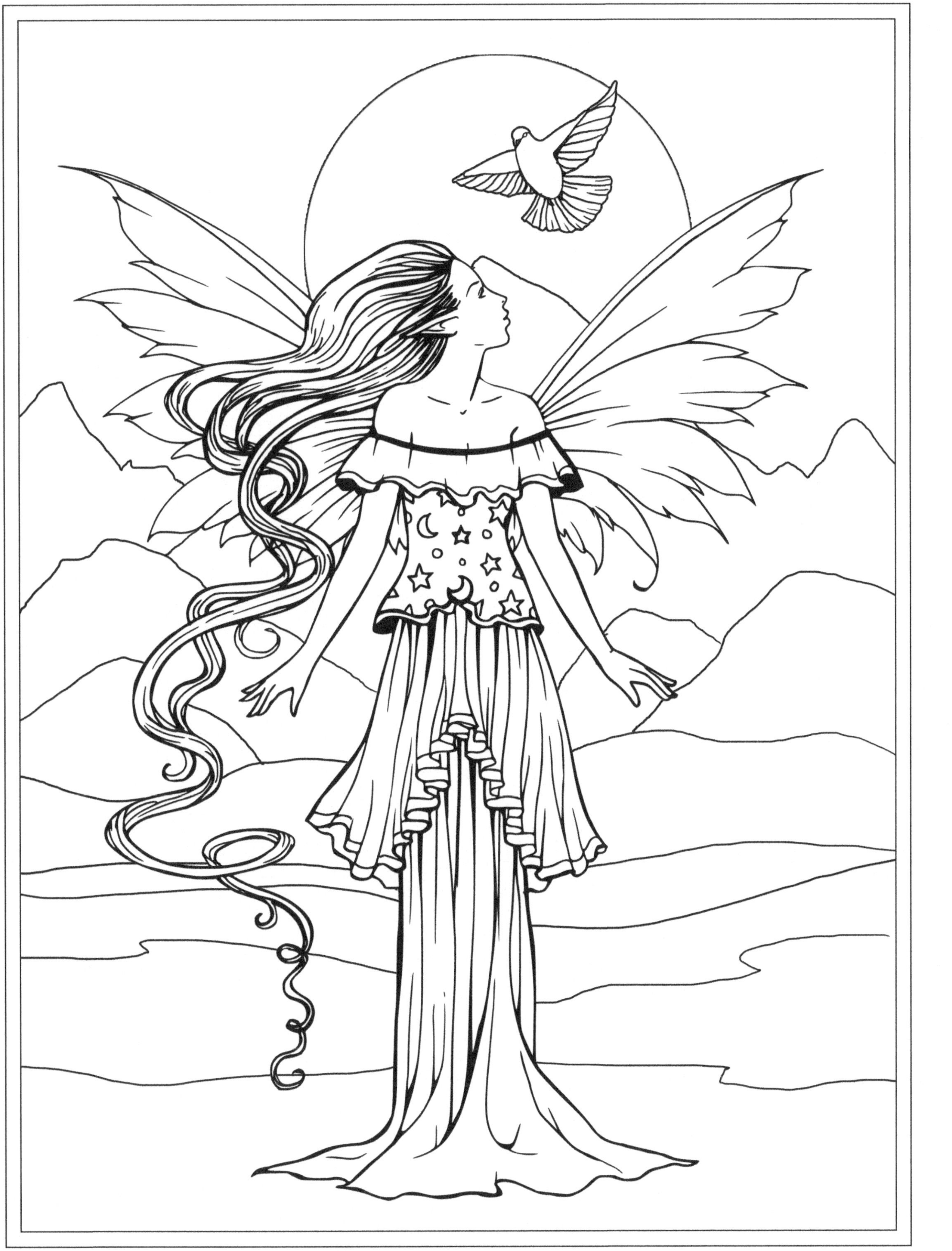

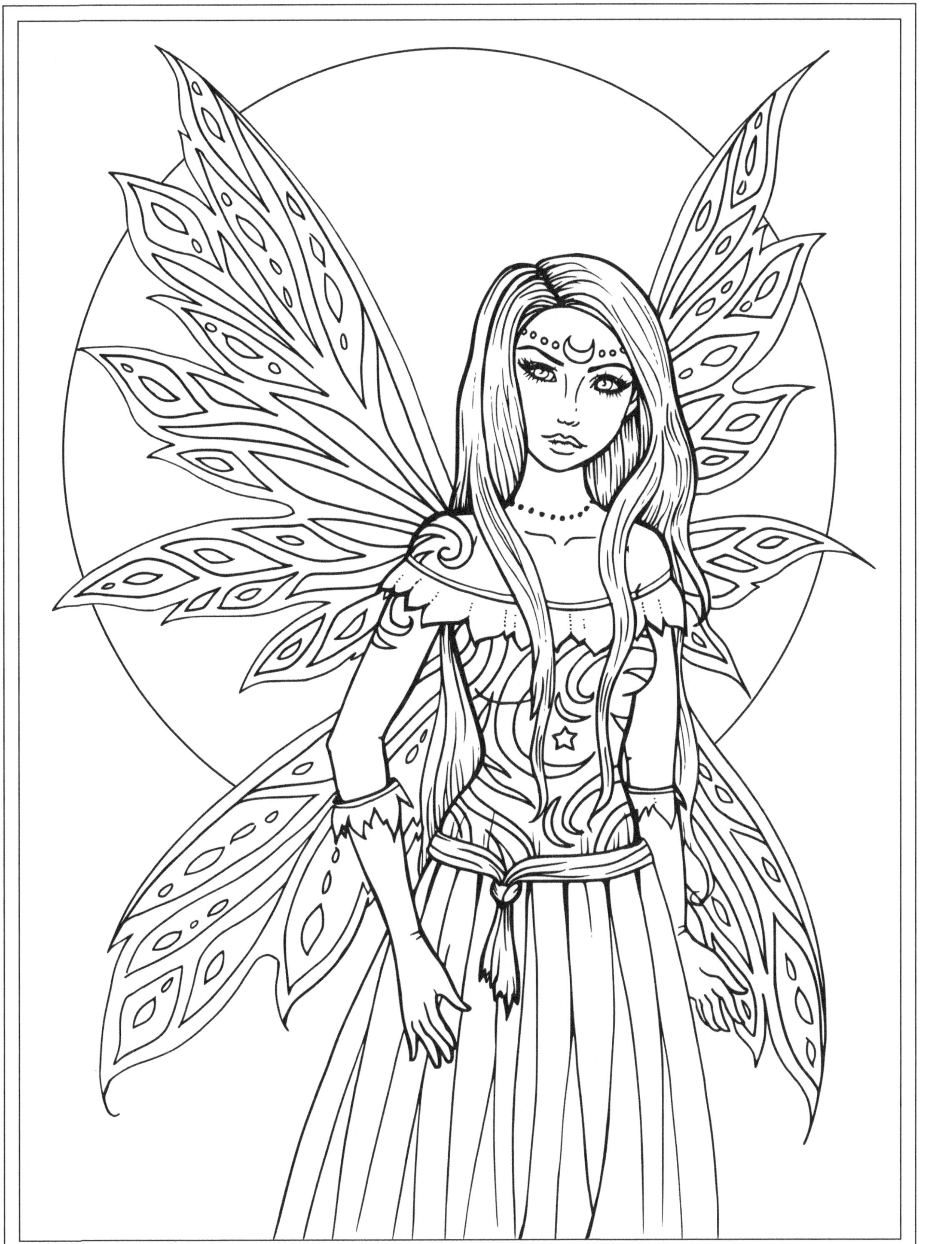

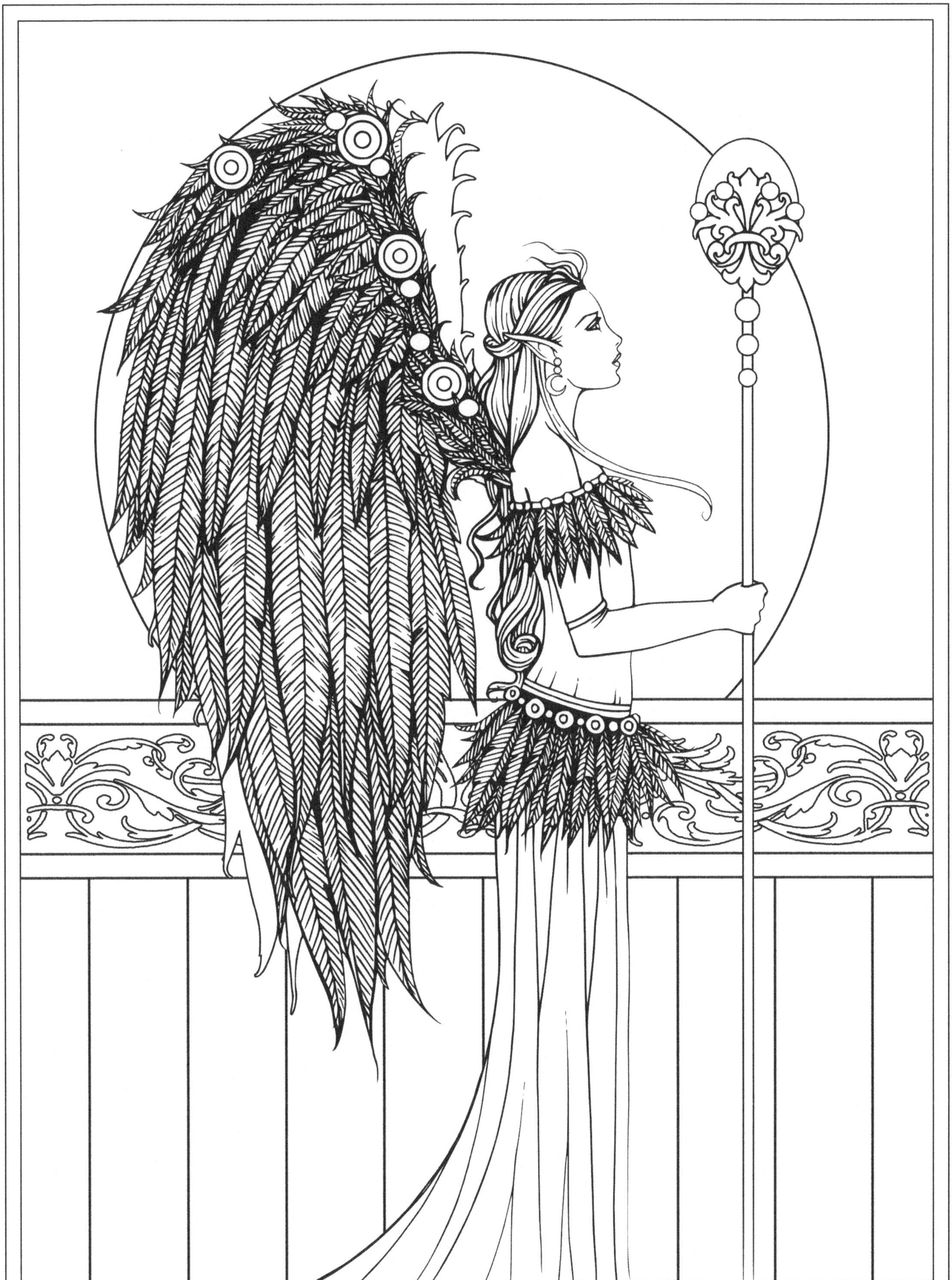

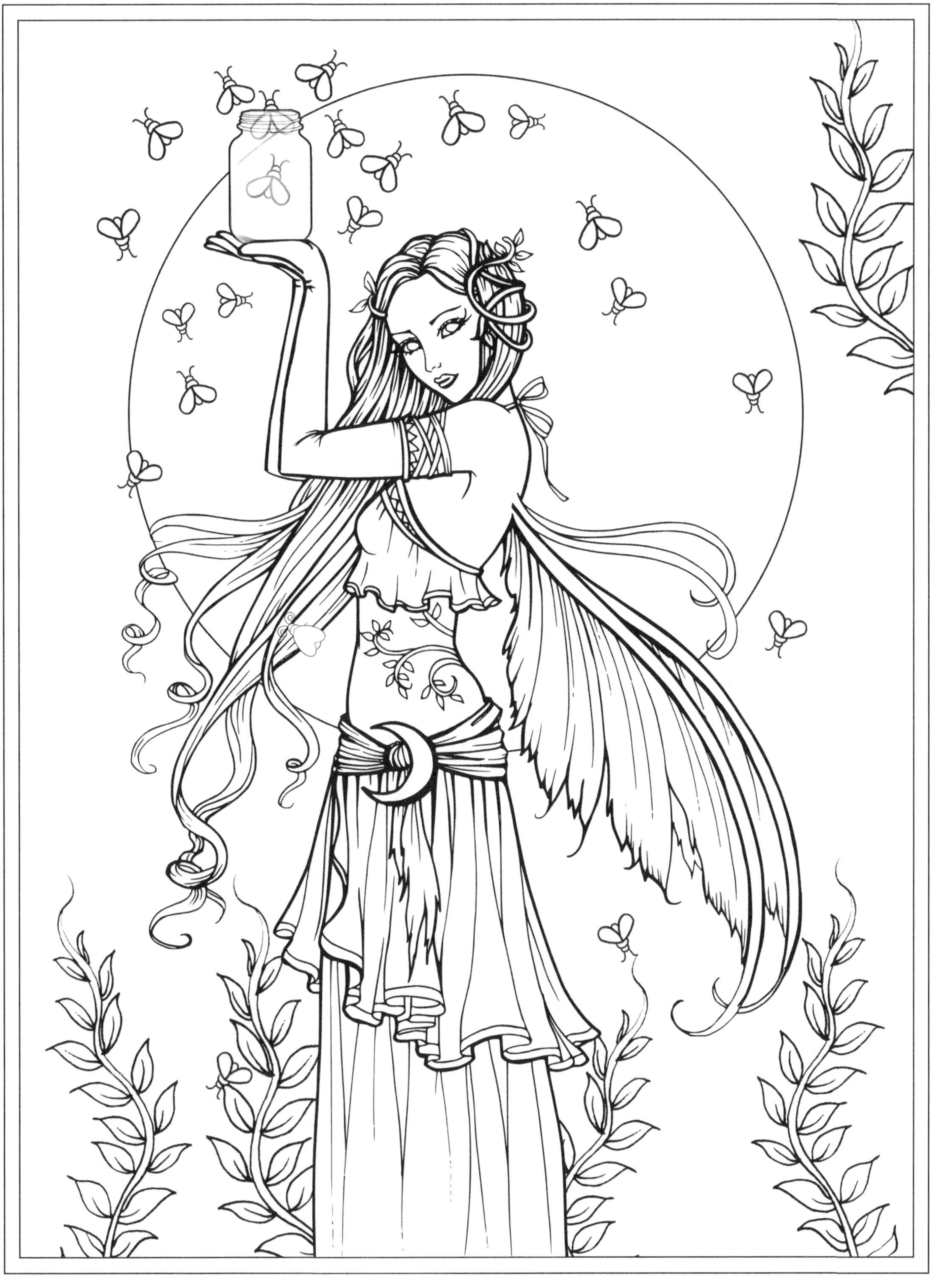

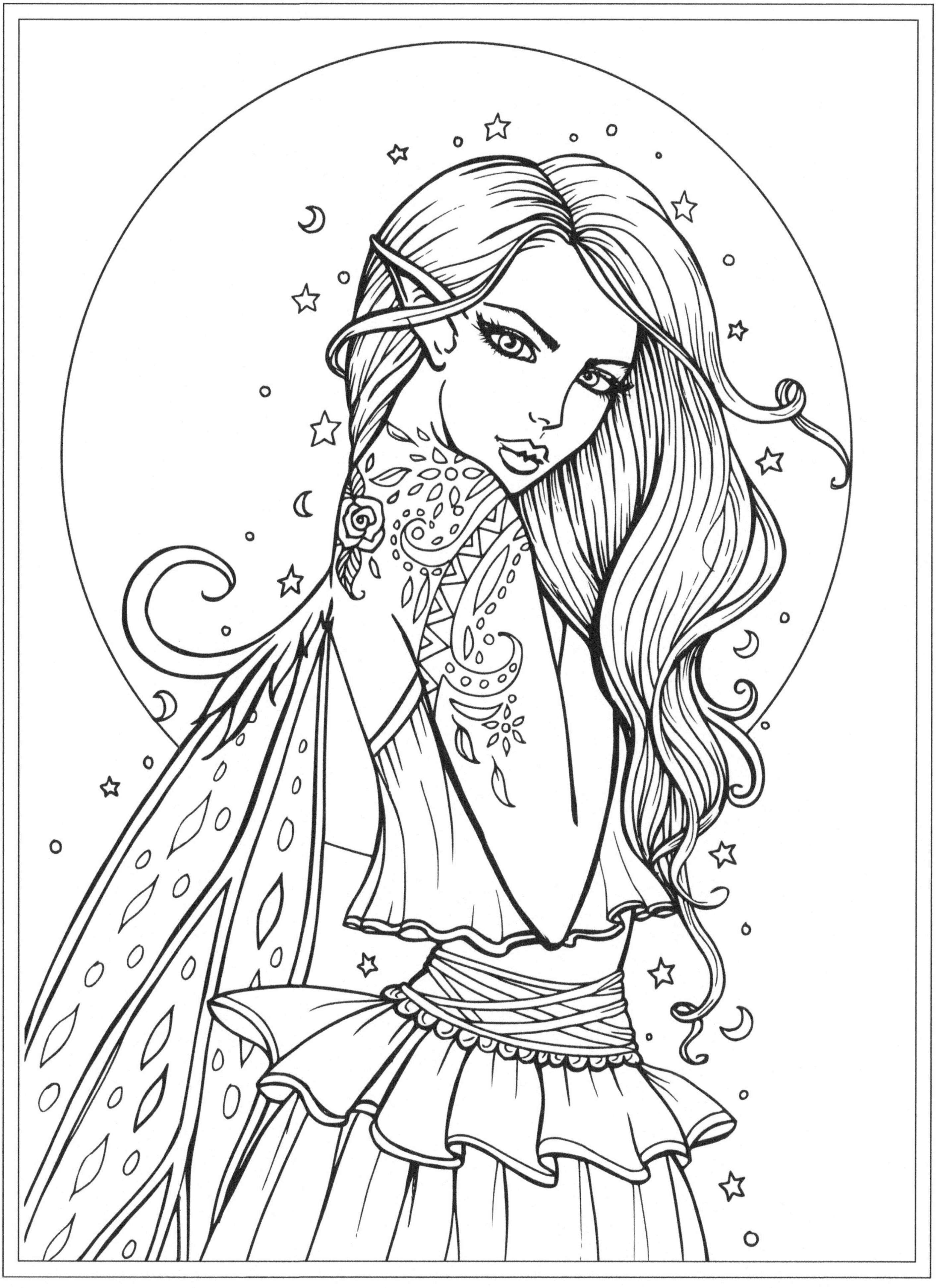

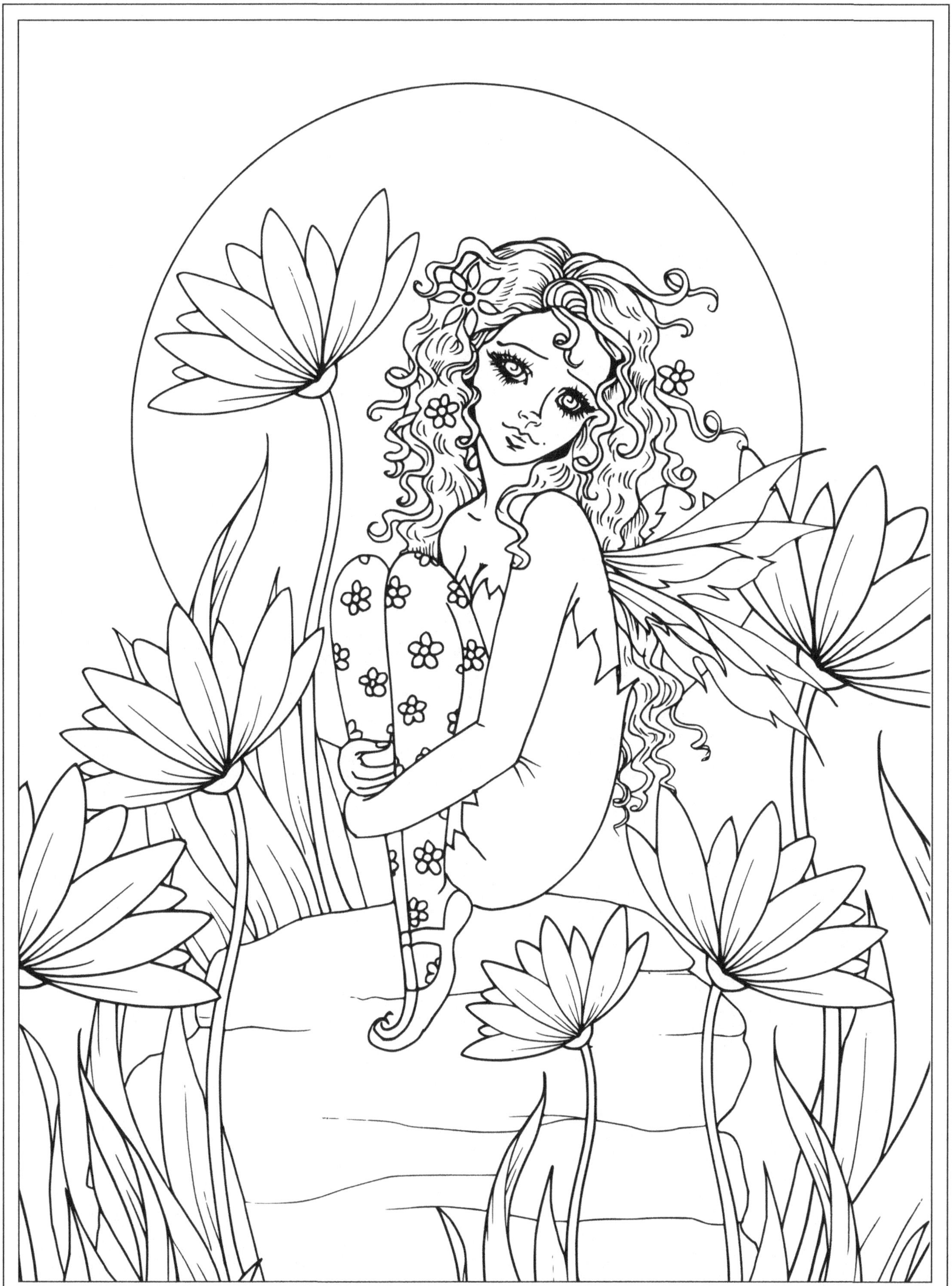

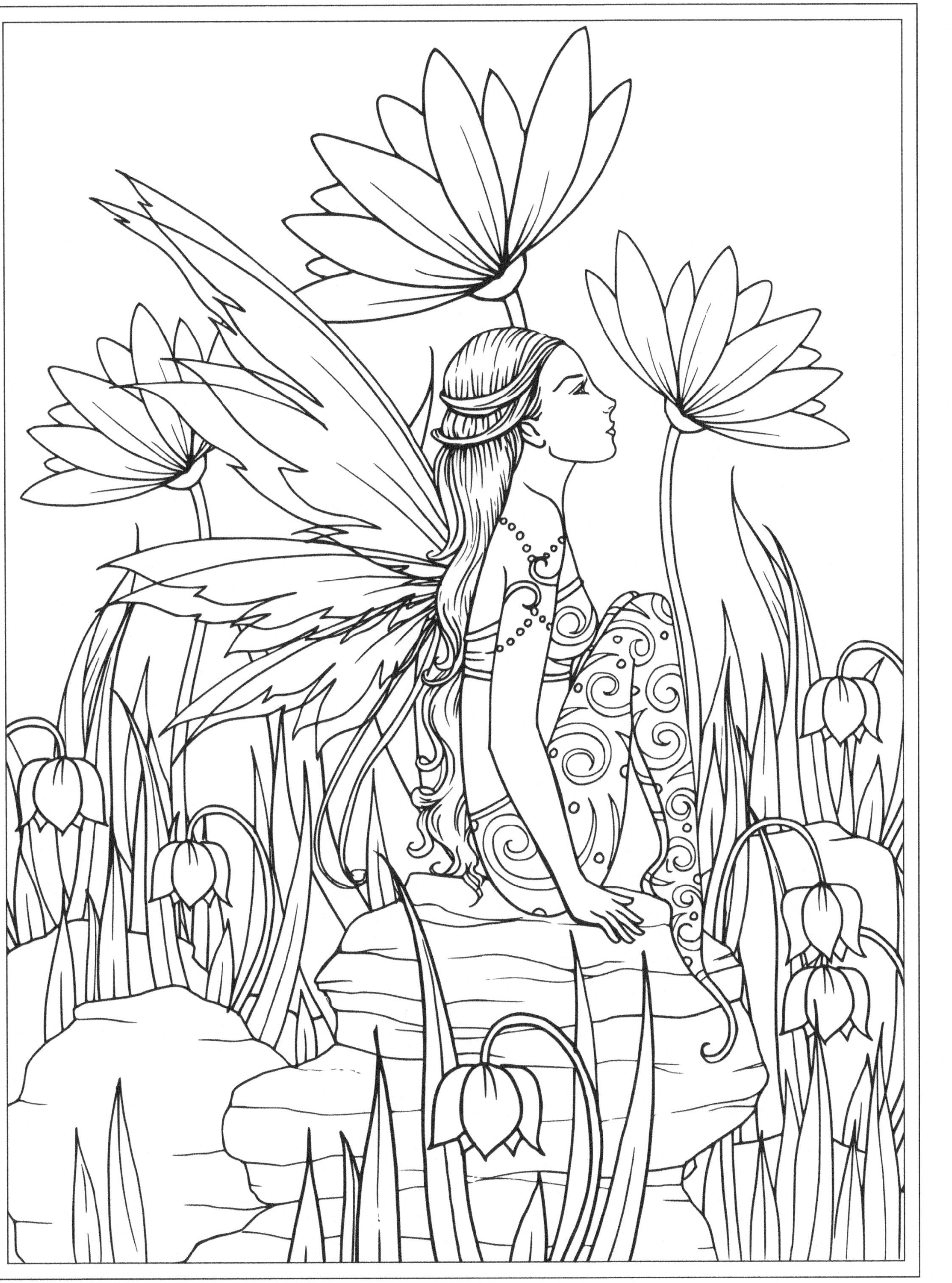

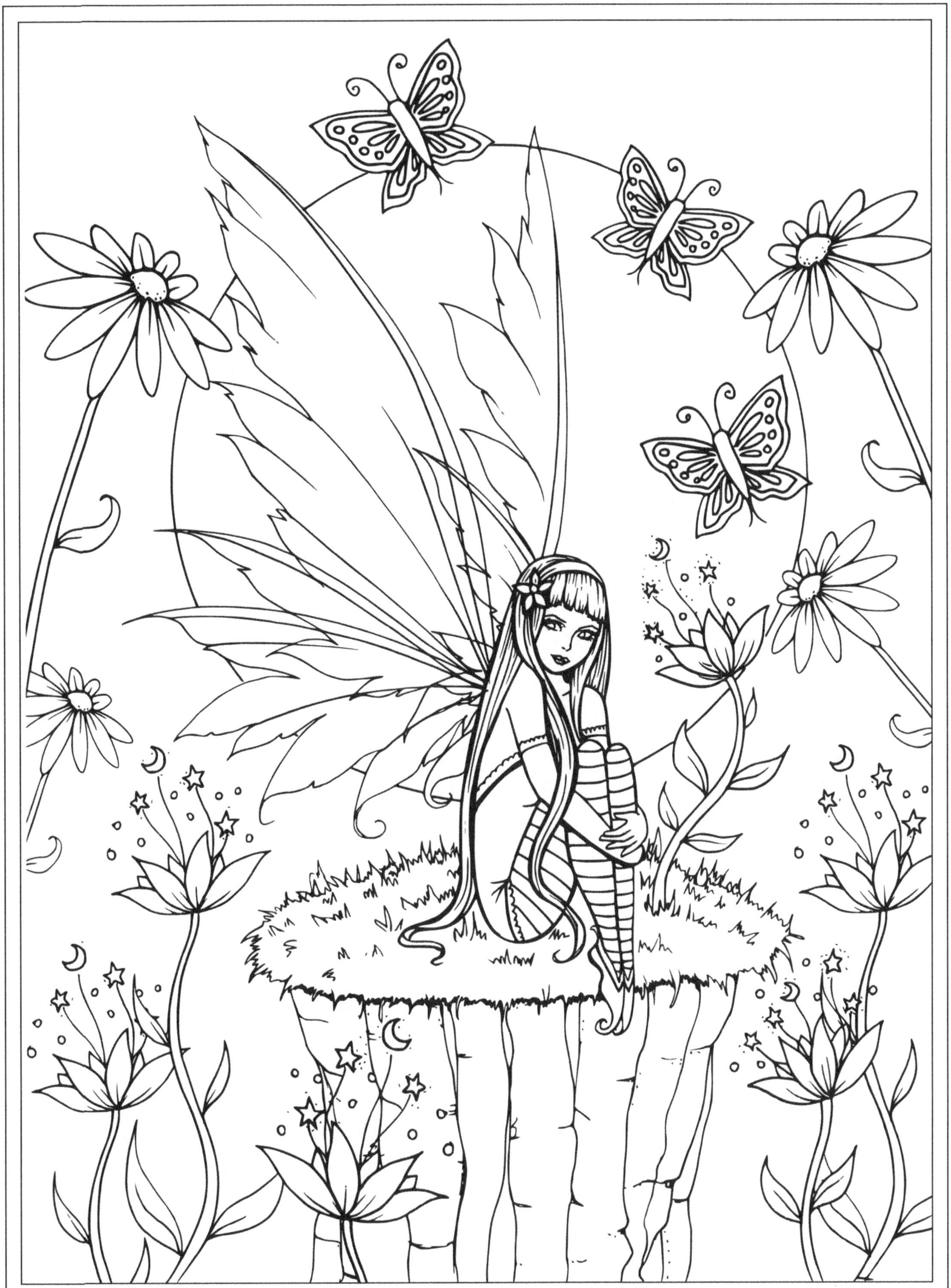

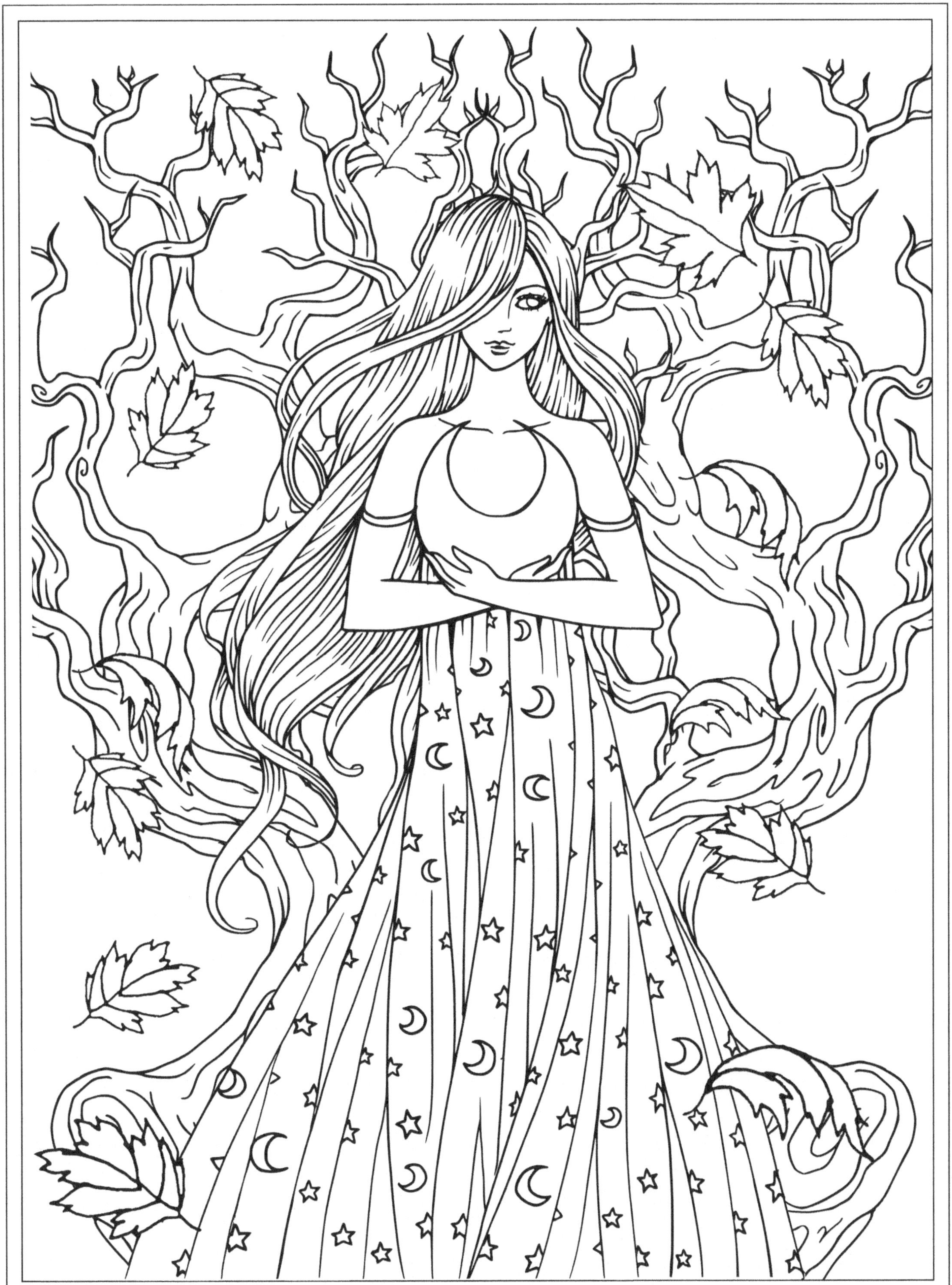

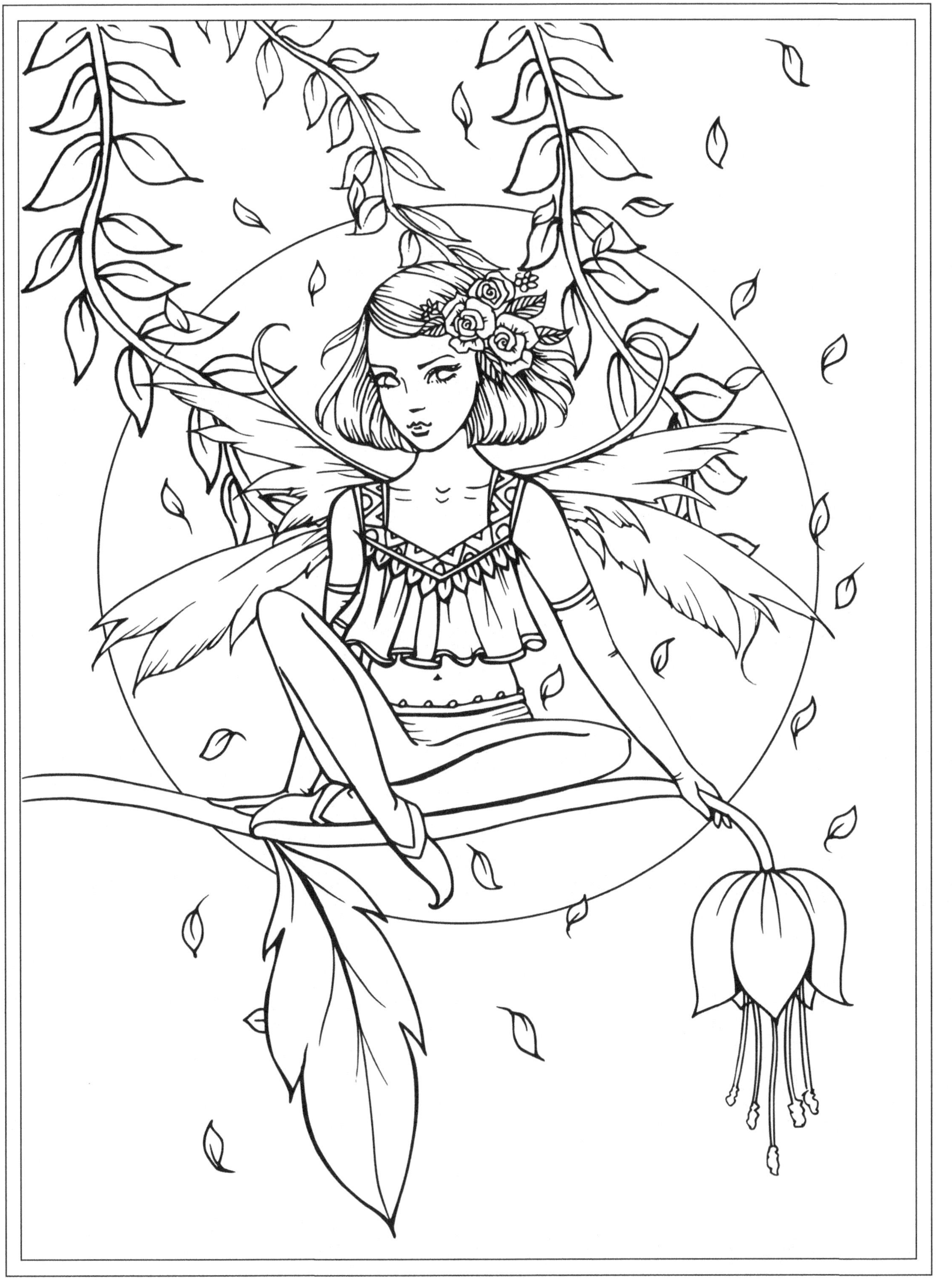

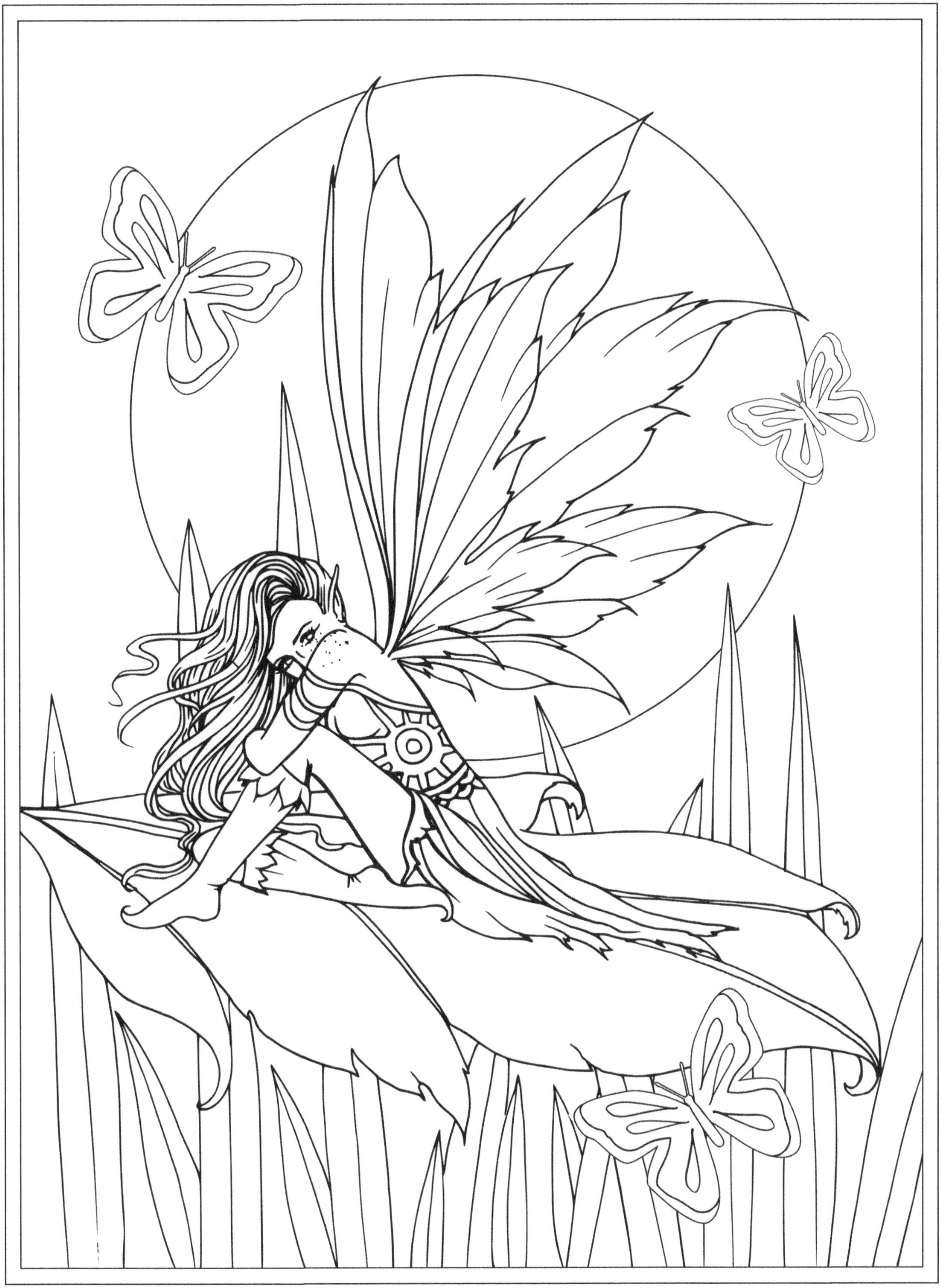

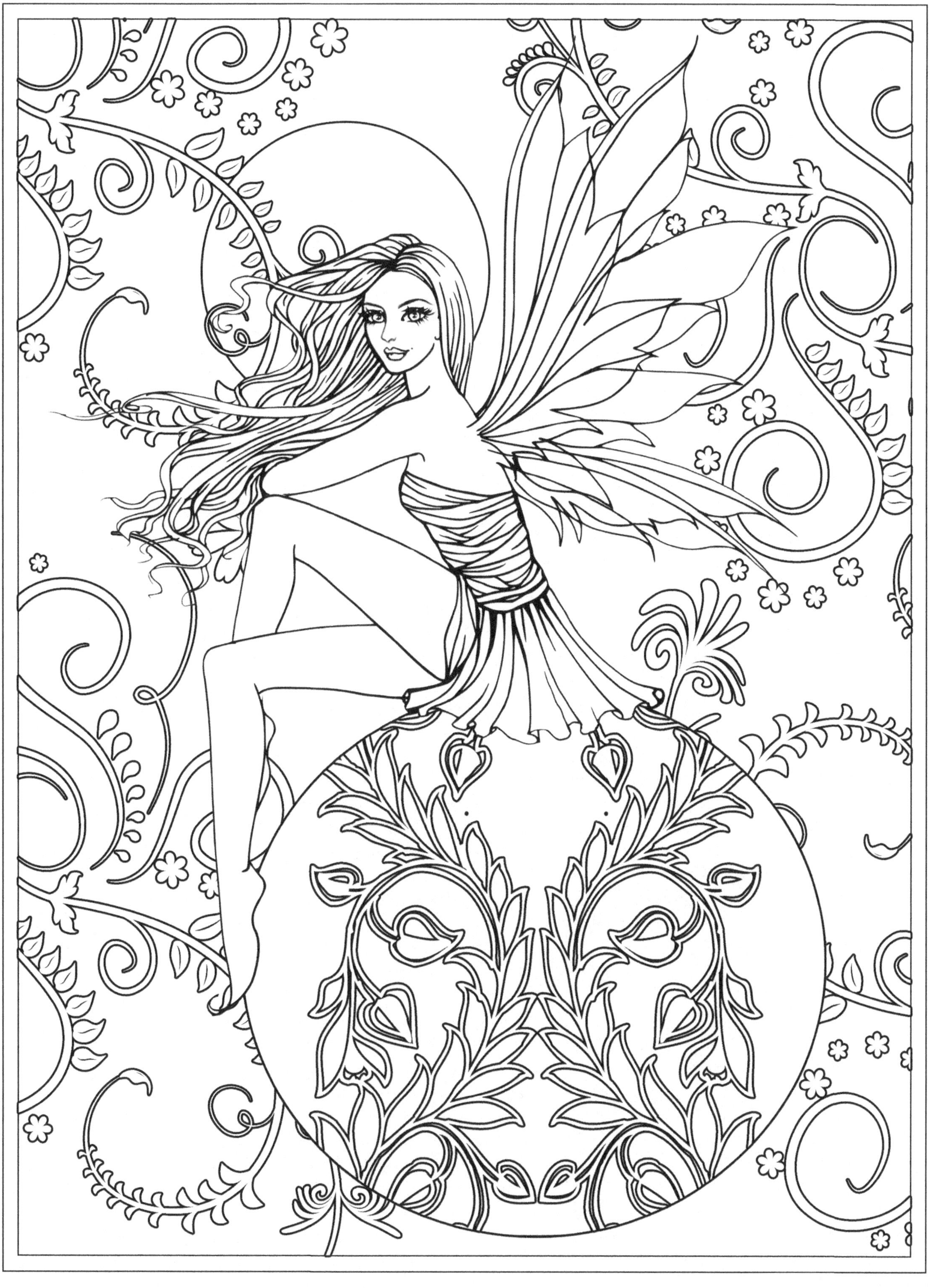

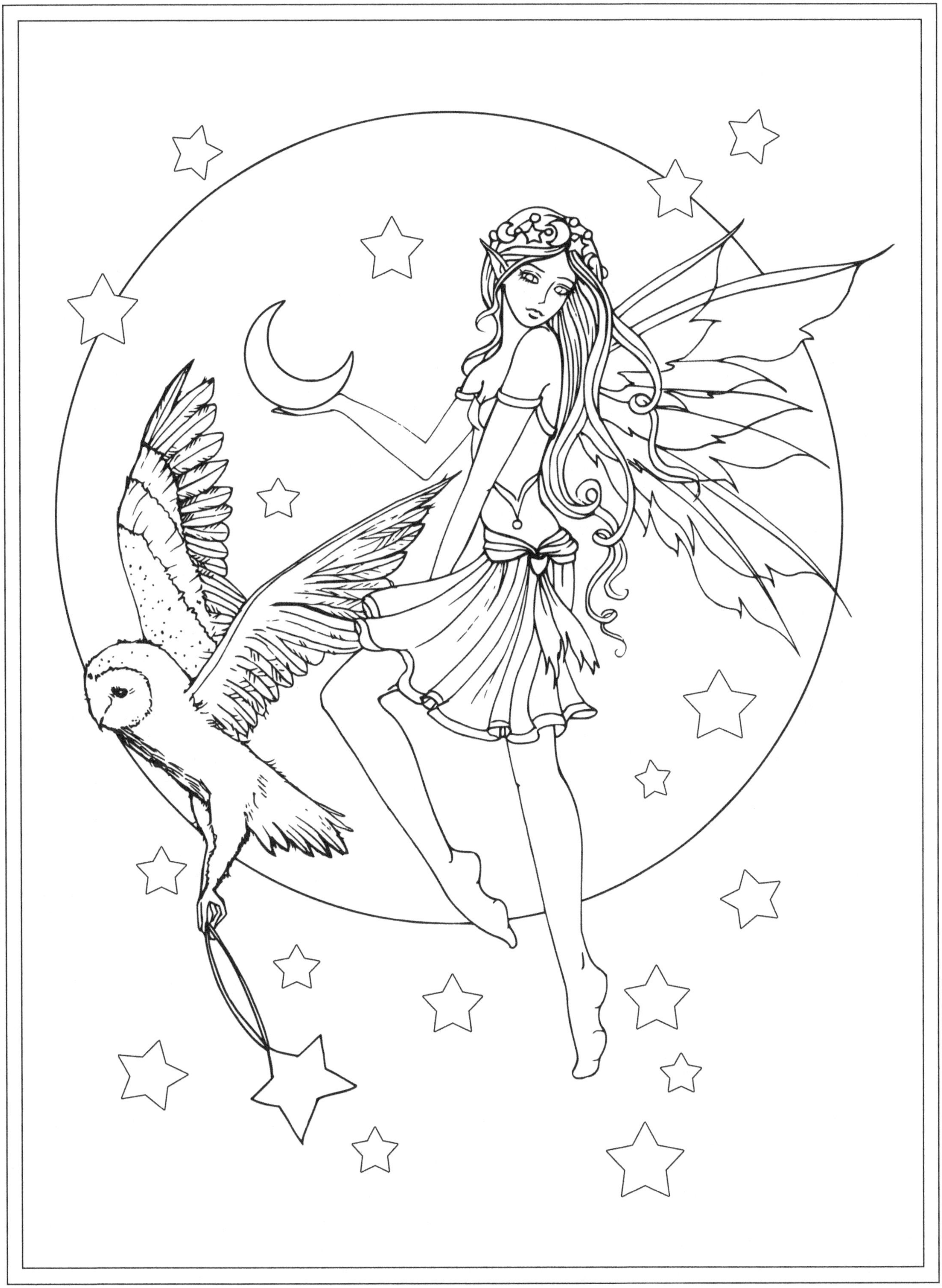

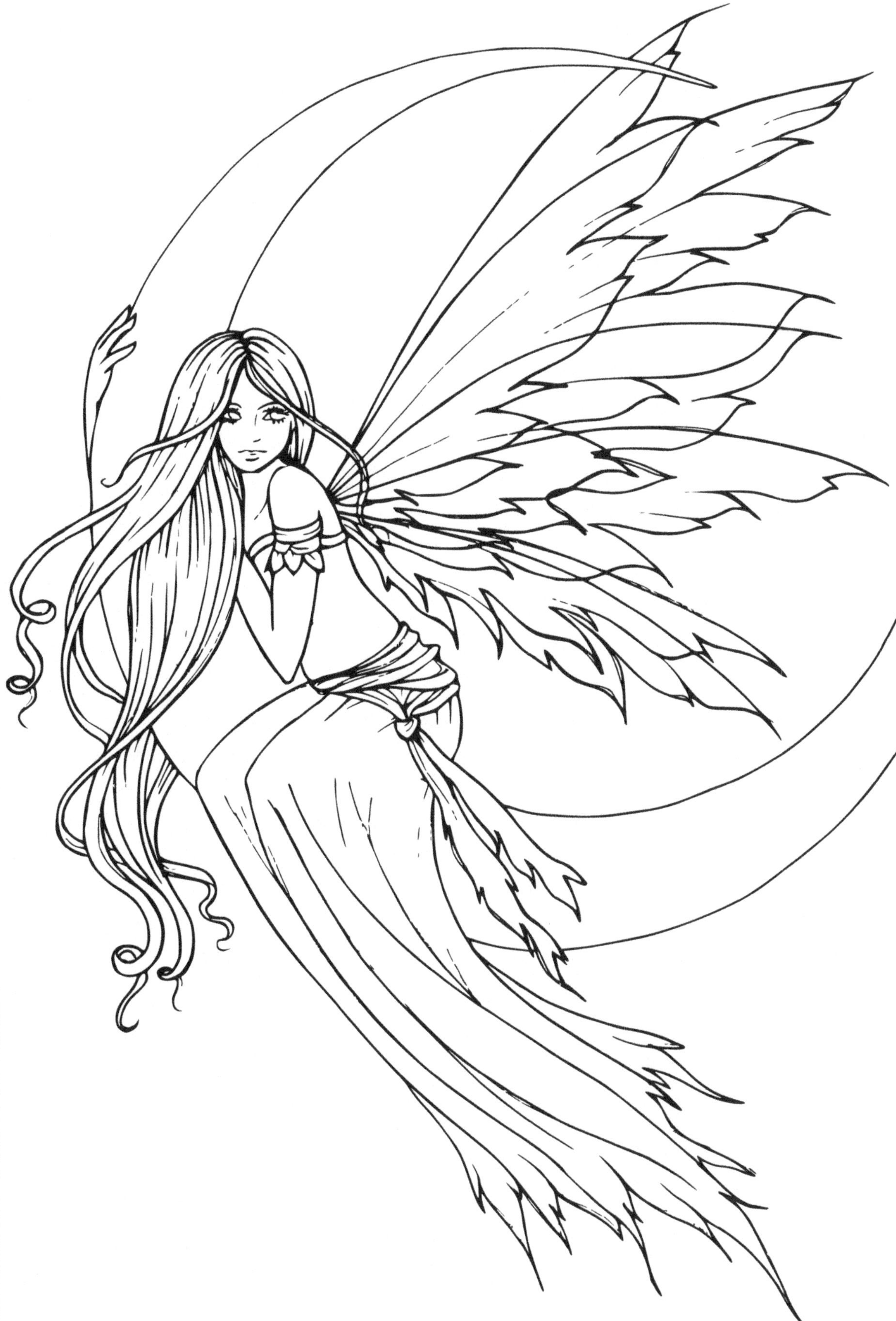

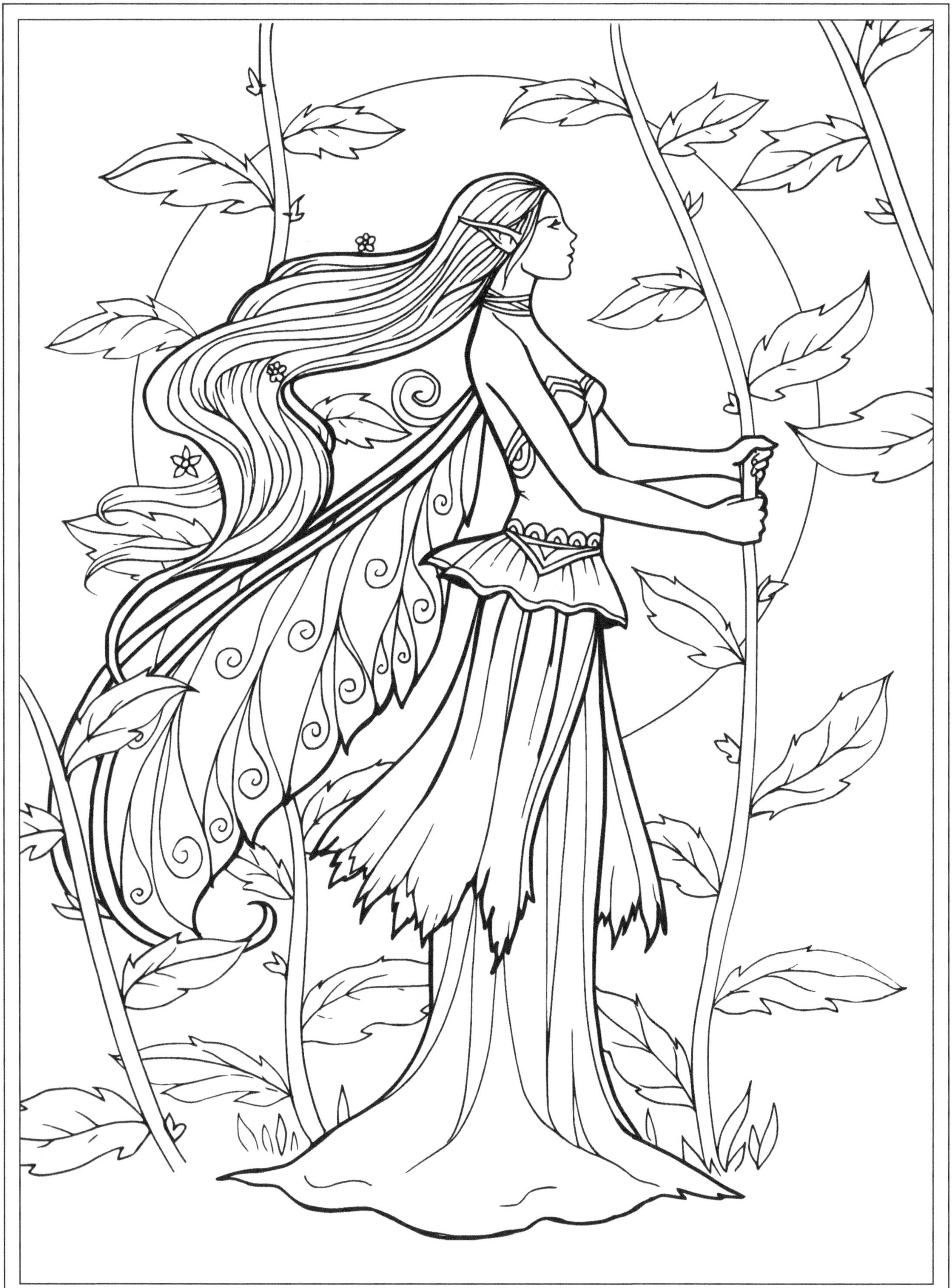

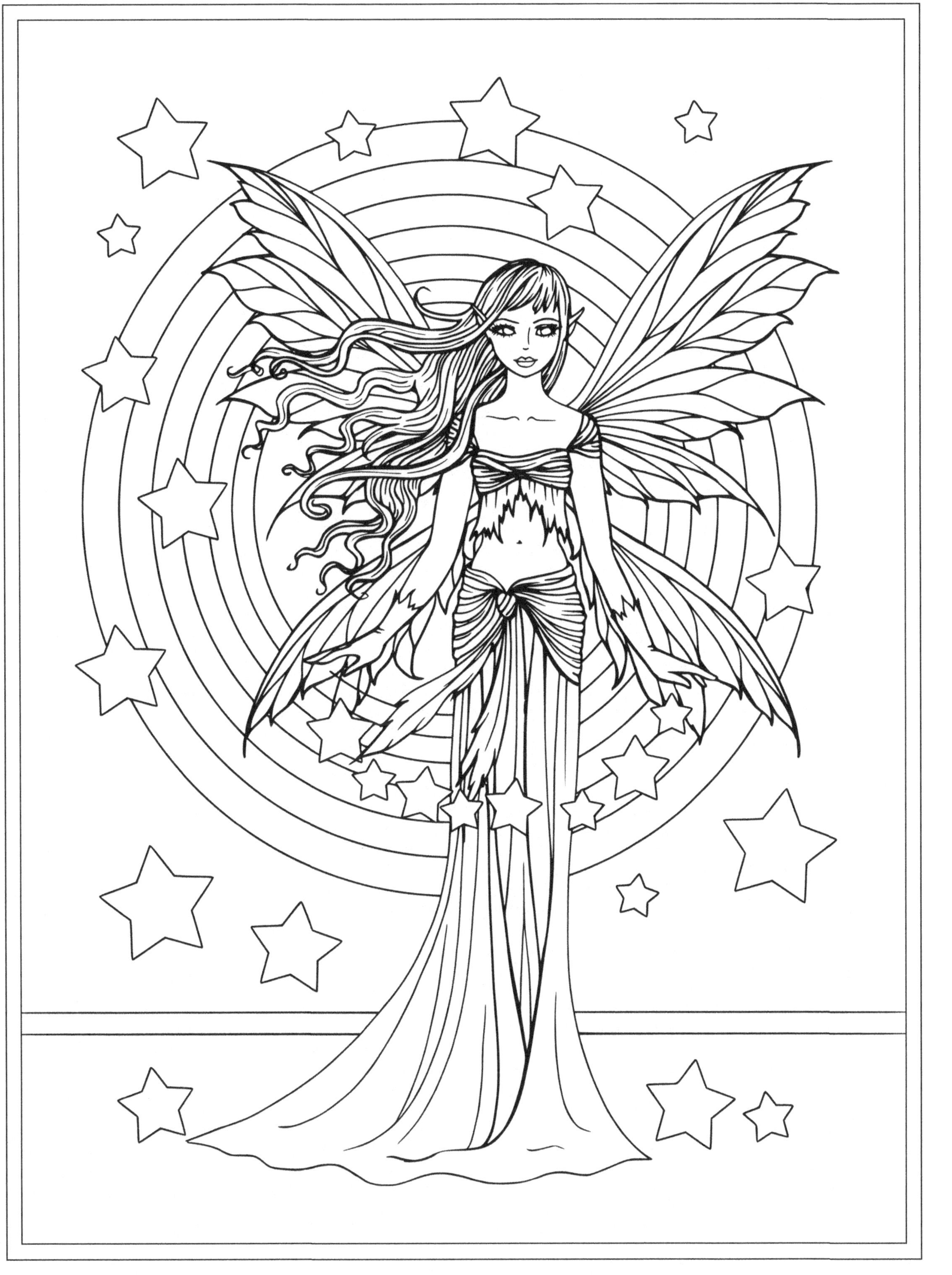

Made in the USA
Middletown, DE
09 December 2021

54813013R00031